HAL•LEONARD
INSTRUMENTAL PLAY-ALONG

CLASSICAL SOLOS
FOR
OBOE

15 Easy Solos for Contest and Performance

Arranged by Philip Sparke

ONLINE MEDIA INCLUDED
Audio Recordings
Printable Piano Accompaniments

PLAYBACK+
Speed • Pitch • Balance • Loop

To access recordings and PDF accompaniments visit:
www.halleonard.com/mylibrary

Enter Code
6136-6741-0637-2724

ISBN 978-1-61780-695-7

HAL•LEONARD®
CORPORATION

7777 W. BLUEMOUND RD. P.O. BOX 13819 MILWAUKEE, WI 53213

Visit Hal Leonard Online at
www.halleonard.com

WALTZ

MORITZ VOGEL
Arranged by PHILIP SPARKE

OBOE

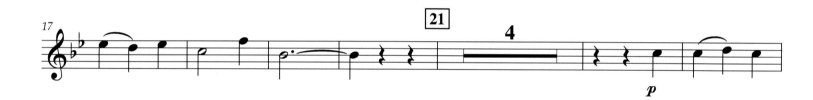

00842543

CHORALE

Now praise, my soul, the Lord

JOHANN SEBASTIAN BACH
Arranged by PHILIP SPARKE

OBOE

00842543

4

HUMMING SONG

from *Album for the Young*

ROBERT SCHUMANN
Arranged by PHILIP SPARKE

OBOE

00842543

GYMNOPÉDIE NO. 1

ERIK SATIE
Arranged by PHILIP SPARKE

OBOE

00842543

I'M CALLED LITTLE BUTTERCUP

from *HMS Pinafore*

SIR ARTHUR SULLIVAN
Arranged by PHILIP SPARKE

OBOE

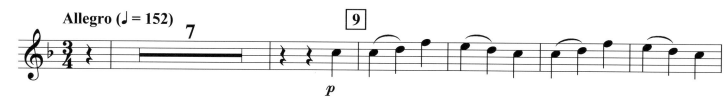

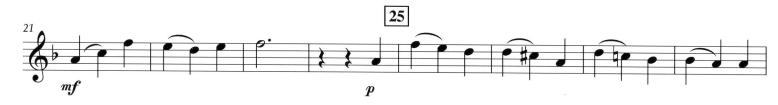

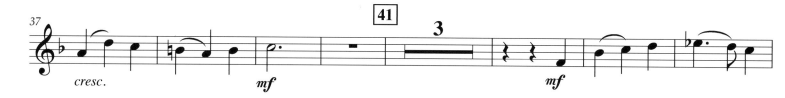

STUDY

Op. 37, No. 3

HENRY LEMOINE
Arranged by PHILIP SPARKE

OBOE

Moderato (♩ = 100)

00842543

MINUET

(Z. 649)

HENRY PURCELL
Arranged by PHILIP SPARKE

OBOE

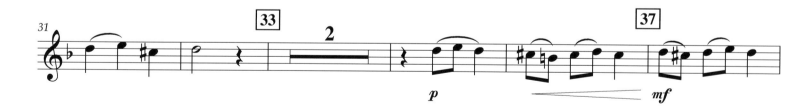

THEME AND VARIATION

from *Sonatina No. 3*

THOMAS ATTWOOD
Arranged by PHILIP SPARKE

OBOE

Moderato (♩ = 104)

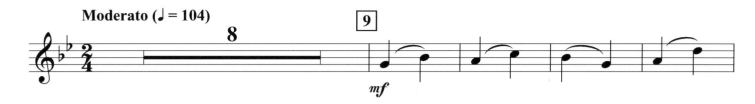

NORTHERN SONG

from *Album for the Young*

ROBERT SCHUMANN
Arranged by PHILIP SPARKE

OBOE

Moderato (♩ = 94)

TWO GERMAN DANCES

from *Twelve German Dances, D. 420*

FRANZ SCHUBERT
Arranged by PHILIP SPARKE

OBOE

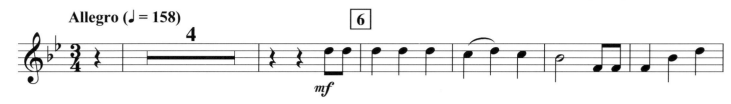

WATCHMAN'S SONG

from *Lyric Pieces, Op. 12*

OBOE

EDVARD GRIEG
Arranged by PHILIP SPARKE

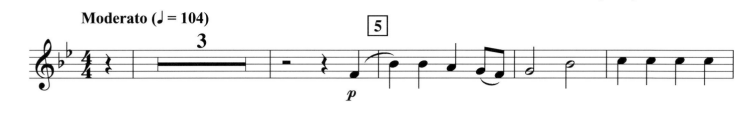

GAVOTTE

JAN LADISLAV DUSSEK
Arranged by PHILIP SPARKE

OBOE

00842543

VIEN QUÀ, DORINA BELLA

ANTONIO BIANCHI
Transcribed by **C. M. von WEBER**
Arranged by PHILIP SPARKE

OBOE

MINUET

from *Notebook for Anna Magdalena Bach*

Attributed to **CHRISTIAN PETZOLD**
Arranged by PHILIP SPARKE

OBOE

Moderato (♩ = 112)

THE PRINCE OF DENMARK'S MARCH

from *Choice Lessons for the Harpsichord or Spinet*

JEREMIAH CLARKE
Arranged by PHILIP SPARKE

OBOE